Table of Contents

Book Description

Quilting is a fun activity that explores the creative ability of an individual. If you wish to give a personalized gift to a loved one that has a part of you and have carefully sewed together to create something exclusive in the truest sense of the word for that individual, then making a quilt is just the thing for you.

It is often said that quilting is both a skill and an art. While selection of patterns, designs, colors and fabrics to put together a piece will test the artist in you, following the multi-step process is a skill, like no other. This book explores the different facets of quilting and throws light on each step you will need to undertake in the process.

Introduction

This book contains proven steps and strategies on how to create a quilt.

Regardless of your skill level, knowledge of quilting or age, quilting is an activity you are sure to enjoy. From every single stitch you place on the quilt to the design and fabric you choose for creating the quilt, every single facet of quilting is an expression of thoughts and emotion. Quilting is an expression of creativity like no other.

A Quilt (Image Courtesy of Robyn Vines Smith)

There are several ways and reasons why quilting is a satisfying and fulfilling activity. Quilting is an activity that helps you create something innovative as well as useful. This makes hand-made quilts an extremely thoughtful gift that the other person will use on a day-to-day basis and remember you all the time. This is also one of the reasons why quilts are kept and cherished for years and through generations, for the sheer sentimental value of the piece.

If you are planning to create a quilt for yourself or for someone you love, you must understand the fact that making a quilt is not just an art, it is also a skill. For some, this activity may seem like an endless activity. There is no doubt that quilting is time-consuming. However, it is the lazy elegance about this art that makes it the leisurely activity it is.

The best thing about quilting is that it is not difficult. Although, quilting requires you to be skillful, it does not require you to be an expert or a master of some extremely tough and hard-to-acquire skills. All in all, quilting is going to take you time, effort and lots of attention. However, when you see the final product of your hard work, you will realize that the activity was worth the effort.

This book is a start-up guide for anyone who is a novice or a beginner to quilting. With every chapter, we help you walk through the difference steps of quilting. All you need to do is walk along, enjoy the journey and use your creativity to adapt the methods and techniques introduced in this book to improve the aesthetic value and usability of your quilts.

Chapter 1: Design - Starting With The Essentials

The process of quilting has gone through several civilizations and generations to give rise to different methods of quilting. Each of these methods impact your end product substantially. Before you decide what method to use, you must keep several factors in mind. The person who is going to use the quilt concerned is the most important factor. The quilt must embody and reflect the personality of this person. Besides this, the use of the quilt and the place where it will be kept and placed also act as determining factors.

Out of all the aesthetic attributes, the most noticeable attribute of the quilt is its color. Choosing the right color for the quilt can go a long way in deciding how good the quilt would turn out for the purpose it was created. For instance, if you are creating a quilt for a child whose room is full of pinks, whites and blues, then a brightly colored quilt may just fit perfectly in the theme.

Once you are done with the color, the next thing you need to figure out in the designing process is whether you are going to make a patchwork quilt or an embroidered quilt. The one to use is more of a personal preference than anything else. When it comes to choosing the pattern for your quilt, you may have to jog the creative side of your brain to draw inspiration from all the things you like and come up with a pattern combination that you can visualize and deem appropriate for the quilt.

In view of the fact you are a beginner, you may face some issues in designing the quilt and visualizing how a pattern or color may look in your final quilt. To help you, you may use some of the quilt kits available in the market to give you some practice and experience. Moreover, scrolling through the quilting pattern sections on the Internet and locally available magazines or books can be a great help and may turn out to be your main source of inspiration.

Long before you start your endeavor, you must clearly understand that even if your first quilt doesn't turn out as expected, you must not get disappointed. The best thing about art is you are not expected to replicate an existing piece. Anything you create is unique and an art piece in its own unique way. No matter what the end product comes out to be, continue trying!

You will be surprised at the ideas you will be able to generate and implement. If you are not confident with working on the quilt fabric right away, you may use paper and pencil to draw sketches of your ideas and improve upon them as you go through design magazines and material.

Patchwork Quilt

One of the most popular quilt types is a patchwork quilt. As the name suggests, several patches of cloth are sewed together to form a pattern and this process is called patchwork. Typically, each quilt is divided into symmetric sections, which are commonly referred to as blocks. Each of these blocks houses a patchwork sequence or pattern in it. Typically, each of these blocks has a similar pattern for symmetry in design. However, if you like, you may vary the design or patchwork pattern by putting in different elements in each of the blocks. You may change the style, shape and arrangement of patches in each of these blocks as per your liking.

Patchwork Quilt (Image Courtesy of Mary Rotman)

Patchwork is both a skill and an art. Therefore, no matter how experienced a quilter you may be, you may make mistakes. While planning to make a patchwork quilt, there are a few things you must keep in mind. First, you must choose the pattern and colors carefully. It is always a good idea to get a second opinion on a pattern or color before finalizing on it. This is particularly the case if you are making the quilt for someone else.

Second, the secret to good patchwork is consistency and matching patterns. Although, having heterogeneity in patterns may seem like an interesting idea, the end product may not turn out to be as appealing as you desire.

Applique Design in Quilts

There are several ways in which you can decorate a fabric. Applique is one of such techniques in which fabrics that are shaped differently are stitched onto one another. This technique is not as simple as it sounds. Therefore, as a beginner, it is always a good idea to start with very simple patterns like simple curves and straight lines.

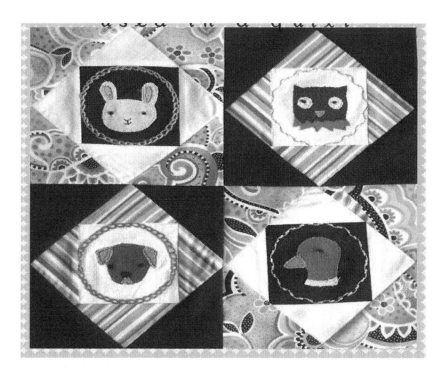

Applique can be done in two fundamental ways. The first method involves the use of the hand to pin applique shapes to one another. For this purpose, shapes are first cut out and held together for the required pattern. This pattern is placed and kept together with the help of pins. You may then sew the shapes together by sewing together threads from the cut shape and the base fabric fixing them into a bond.

The fusible adhesive method is the second type of applique that is commonly done. As the name suggests, fusible adhesive is used to attach the shapes to the foundation fabric. According to the standard process, shapes are cut out. Then, fusible adhesive is cut out of similar shapes. This fusible adhesive is placed between the shaped fabric and the foundation fabric. To attach the two surfaces together, the three layers are carefully leveled together and ironed.

To make the fixture permanent, you may stitch the ends by hand or machine, giving your applique a good finish. If you are not good or comfortable with hand or machine stitching, you may also use craft glue for this purpose. Although, this method will solve your purpose, it will not get you the finish and authenticity that the hand method helps you achieve.

Using Embroidery

When you use stitches on a fabric to create a decorative pattern, the thread work is called embroidery. The stitching done for this purpose can be done either by machine or hand. Besides this, you may use silk threads, metallic threads, embroidery floss and colored threads to achieve different effects in your pattern.

Embroidery is one of the oldest techniques used for creating pictures and patterns on fabric with the help of strands of threads that are sewed onto the fabric in an intricate manner. Like we mentioned before, a quilt is typically divided into blocks. Patterns are embroidered onto these blocks with the help of cotton, silk or woolen threads. There are many types of stitches that are used to create different types of patterns. Embroidery can also be used to enhance an existing patch quilt adding to the aesthetic value of the patches placed in the blocks of the quilt.

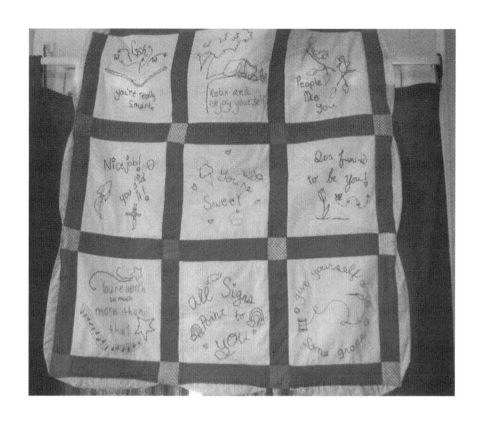

Embroidery Quilt (Image Courtesy of Dana)

While nothing creates an authentic pattern like embroidery, it is not an easy task to accomplish in view of the fact that embroidering a pattern onto a fabric is laborious and requires immense patience and skill. To reduce the difficulty levels of embroidery and make it more accessible to one and all, several machines and tools have been developed. You may explore these

options if embroidering by hand is an uphill task for
you.

Chapter 2: How to Choose Color, Fabric and Pattern

Once you have finalized the design, you have a fair idea of what you want to make and how you expect it to look. Therefore, the next thing that you need to do is to pick a pattern for your quilt. After you are done with this, you will need to finalize the type, color and nature of fabrics that you wish to use for your quilt. This chapter shall explore these facets of quilt making.

Choosing the Fabric

When it comes to choosing the fabric for creating your quilt, the most important facet of the fabric you need to pay attention to is the purpose you are creating the quilt for. This is perhaps the reason why you will notice excessive use of cottons and cotton-mixes in quilt making. The versatility, strength, anti-allergic and non-flammable characteristics of this fabric are the fundamental reasons why cotton and its mixes make for a good quilting fabric.

If you have chosen a colorful pattern that requires a bright foundation fabric, you are likely to be tempted by synthetic fabrics. However, before you decide to pick them, be sure to understand these fabrics crease much more and are extremely difficult to quilt, particularly in light of the fact that you are still a beginner. Therefore, for now, using cotton is recommended. As you gain experience, working with spongy fabrics like synthetics may also become easier for you.

If you are using a colored fabric, ensure the colors are fast and will not bleed when washed. In addition, do not use a 'too heavy' or 'too light' fabric. Fabrics that are too heavy, like denim, is extremely difficult to quilt. Similarly, fabrics like organza are too flimsy for quilting and do not make a good fit for this purpose.

Choosing Color of the Foundation Fabric

Regardless of whether you are choosing the color of the foundation fabric or the pattern you plan to put in the quilt blocks, the most important thing you need to consider is the mood and purpose of the quilt concerned. Although, keeping in mind the person the quilt is being made for is important, remember to visualize how the quilt will look to you, had you been using it.

Most people who create a quilt for a friend or loved one generally try to use something of sentimental value to the receiver of the gift in the quilt. For example, they may use a patch from their favorite old dress or granny's handkerchief, adding an element of thoughtfulness to the quilt.

While choosing colors, also remember the fact that some colors like yellows and reds are warm colors. These colors are appropriate for use in lounges as they tend to add alertness and activity to the aura of the room. On the other hand, colors like greens and browns are cool colors. These colors are used in bedrooms or rooms meant for resting.

Cutting and Designing Templates

Now that you have the raw materials ready, and you are all set to start quilting, you need to design your templates. If you plan to create a quilt that is just made of squares, then you will not need any templates. All you need to do is use the rotary board and cutter to get perfect squares from your fabric. This is also true for patchwork designs.

On the other hand, if you plan to create a quilt with applique designs with different shapes, you will need to cut out templates for the shapes you intend to use. For cutting out the templates, you will again need the rotary cutter and board. However, ensure you use different rotary cutters for fabric and template boards for the simple reason that using cutters on hard surfaces like boards blunts the blade. You may use any of the different applique techniques for transferring designs from the template to the fabric.

Marking and cutting the fabric is one of the steps you have to take since you cannot afford making mistakes as a result of the sheer criticality of the step. If you make any mistakes in marking or cutting the fabric, the overall appearance of the quilt will be significantly impacted. First things first, you need to get the right fabric marker for yourself.

Testing the fabric marker before actually using it on your fabric for marking your design is highly recommended. In order to test your fabric marker, you can cut out a corner of the fabric that you intend to use for your quilt. Next, make marks on this test fabric. These marks must be similar to the marks you will be making in your actual design.

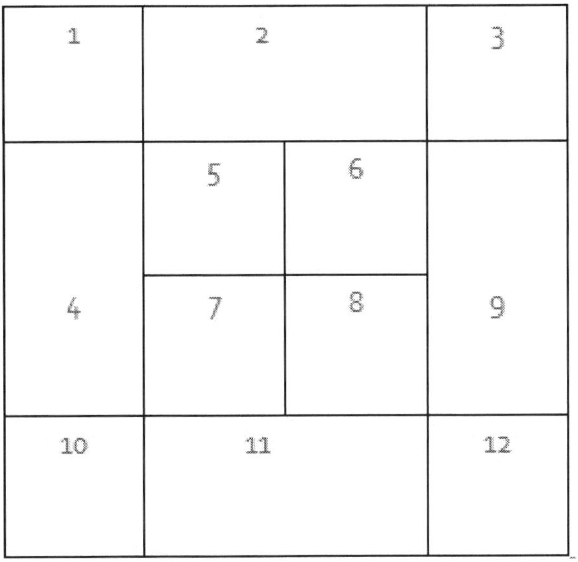

1	2	3
4	5 / 6	9
	7 / 8	
10	11	12

You can use the pattern shown above to cut your fabric. Even though 2, 4, 9 and 11 are same size, do not interchange their position for the simple reason that no matter how perfectly you cut them out, they will fit perfectly only in the places from which and for which they have been cut. Also, cut the vertical pieces for 4 and 9, while you cut horizontal pieces for 2 and 11. There are several other patterns that can be used. The pattern shown above has been kept here for its sheer simplicity.

Whenever you choose the fabric for creating templates, be sure to use the exact fabric. Using scrap fabric for the templates will not help you visualize the final product so well. Besides this, washing the sample fabric will also tell if the marker tags will go away or not. If you use a different fabric, you will not be able to estimate this facet accurately.

Lastly, remember to use sharp scissors for cutting out the templates. Blunt scissors usually tear off the edges spoiling the fabric shape completely. Keep the blocks in order so it will be easier for you to assemble your quilt as described in the next section.

Chapter 3: Assembling the Quilt Blocks and Top

Assembling the blocks of the quilt is a complicated process and largely depends on the type of quilt you are making. For instance, if you are making a patchwork quilt, you need to start with the centerpiece and sew the outer pieces in layers, layer after layer. On the other hand, if you're planning to make an applique quilt, you will have to plan out your design and layout process.

For the planning process, you must keep in mind the stenciling plan. For example, if you plan to create a tree, you must start with the tree trunk, then create the branches and put the leaves on the branches as part of the last stage. Planning out this process well before you start will ease your pain in view of the fact that you will need to repeat this process over and over again before your full quilt is ready.

How to Assemble Quilt Blocks

Assuming you are creating the same design of the quilt as shown in the previous chapter. The basic elements of the design are as follows:

1. Blocks 2, 4, 9 and 11 are of the same size (rectangular) with the difference being that 2 and 11 are horizontally aligned while 4 and 9 are vertically aligned.

2. Blocks 1, 3, 5, 6, 7, 8, 10 and 12 are of the same size (square) with the difference being that 1, 3, 10, 12 are positioned on the four corners while 5, 6, 7 and 8 form the central piece.

In order to assemble the blocks together, you need to follow the instructions given below.

1. The first step is to sew 5 and 6 together.

2. The second step is to sew 7 and 8 together.

3. Sew 1, 2 and 3 blocks together.

4. Sew 10, 11 and 12 blocks together.

5. Now, sew the 5-6 block with the 7-8 block.

6. Sew 4 and 9 blocks to the block combination received as a result of step 5.

7. Now, sew the block combinations received as a result of step 3, step 6 and step 4 (top to bottom) to get the pattern shown in the figure.

While you sew the blocks together, be sure to keep the following things in mind.

- Ensure you sew the right sides together.
- Sew with strands close to each other to keep the fabric from slacking.
- Once you have sewed two blocks together, press the seam. This will help you align the blocks properly.
- Also, while you press the seam, be sure to maintain the same direction of pressing. If you are pressing right to left, follow this pattern throughout the process.

How to Assemble Quilt Top

After you have the blocks assembled, the next step is to stitch the quilt blocks together. This is generally done with the help of a process called sashing. As a result of the process, each of your blocks will receive a border and give the whole quilt a simpler and uncomplicated appearance. From a design point of view, sashing allows the viewer to notice the intricate details of each block without getting lost in the complicacy of the whole quilt.

Sashing is cut in the form of long strips, which are sewed onto the block boundaries in the manner shown in the figure. There are several ways in which the sashing ends are sewn together. However, the best way is to sew them at right angles, as shown in the figure. This allows your quilt to have a symmetric geometrical shape.

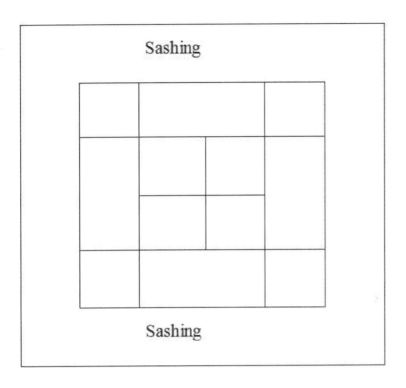

Like with the block assembly, you will need to press the seam after sewing the sashing with the blocks. When you do so, be sure to press matching seams in opposite directions. Also, if your quilt is made from a combination of light and dark fabrics, press from the dark fabric to the light one. If you do otherwise, the seam will be clearly visible and the look of the quilt will be affected.

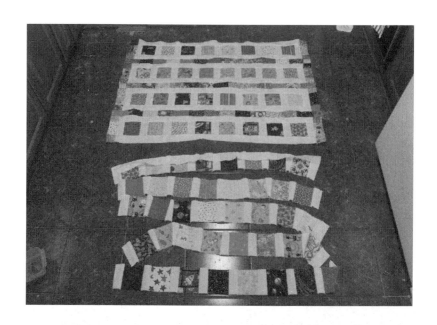

Chapter 4: Choosing Quilt Batting

After you have your quilt top ready, ironed and seamed, it is time to look at the batting. The quilt is typically made up of three layers. While we are done with the quilt top, which is the first layer of the quilt, we are yet to talk about the other two layers. The lower layer is the quilt base and the middle or sandwiched layer comprises of the padding or batting layer.

Several types of batting are available, each of them varying in texture, thickness and composition. You may choose a woolen, cotton or synthetic batting on the basis of your requirements and preferences. Here are the main characteristics of each type of batting and the purpose they are deemed best fit for.

Cotton Batting

Cotton is a natural fiber, which is the easiest to work around and experiment with. Moreover, getting an even look with this material is much easier than any other material. This is perhaps the reason why cotton batting is considered best for beginners and small projects.

Polyester Batting

If you are looking for a lightweight and inexpensive alternative to cotton, polyester is a good pick. It gives the quilt a comfortable puffiness. However, this material suffers from some inherent drawbacks. One of the most profound drawbacks is the fact that this material is too fine and can weave through the fabric to come out of the quilt.

Wool Batting

If you are making a quilt to be used for excessively cold climates, you may take the wool batting for a warmer quilt. This material is flat and lacks the puffiness of synthetic materials. However, wool is delicate and you will need to take care of washing instructions and maintenance guidelines during use.

This puts durability and ease of use of the quilt in question.

Factors to Consider

The two main factors you need to consider while choosing the batting for your quilt are thickness and size. The thicker the batting of the quilt, the heavier it will become and the more difficult it will be for people to use it. Therefore, the use of a light batting is recommended. However, if you are making the quilt for use in very cold climates, then a heavier batting may be required. A good workaround to keep the weight of the quilt in check is to use extra padding tied to the quilt instead of increasing the thickness of the batting in the quilt. In addition to the weight issue, it is equally important to understand that sewing a heavy batting quilt will be much more difficult and tiresome. It is much easier to bring the needle and thread through the thin batting than a heavy batting.

When it comes to deciding the size of the batting, as a general rule, the batting is sized bigger than the quilt top. However, the size must not exceed the size of the back fabric. This allows you some extra fabric, which can be sewn back together in case you need to pull a bit of fabric to accommodate the fabric and yet maintain the size of the quilt.

If you are making a large quilt, you may have to combine batting together. You may also use saved batting from previously created quilts to put the piece together. These pieces are tucked together by loose stitches, which are used for just holding the pieces together. Moreover, ensure no two pieces overlap with each other. It is double the thickness of the batting in some areas, making the batting uneven.

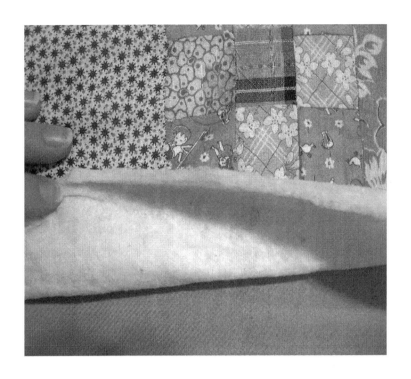

Chapter 5: Choosing Quilt Backing and Binding

Now that you have the two layers of the quilt ready, it is time to turn the last layer, backing. It is a general practice that people spend most of their time arranging the top of the quilt and do not pay enough attention to the backing or the binding process. There are no two ways about the fact that the quilt top is the most visible part of the quilt and thus the most important. However, it does not take away the fact that backing is just as essential.

Traditionally, a white-colored cotton or cotton-mix fabric is used for backing. You may use the color you like or the color that matches well with the colors in your quilt to give a balanced look to your quilt. Moreover, you may choose the fabric you like, but be sure to check if the backing fabric is comfortable enough for the person to sleep with.

Another important thing to consider while choosing the color and print of your backing fabric is that the color and print must not be too bright and overpowering. Try to choose a simple print or plain fabric or else the backing fabric might just overpower your quilt top. There can be just one star in the show. If you want your quilt top to steal the show, you will have to use subtle design and color for your backing fabric. As a rule, always match a bright-colored quilt top with a dull-colored anterior.

Creating a Two-Sided Quilt

Keeping in view the multi-utility of quilts, you can treat the quilt backing as another quilt top. However, ensure you don't use a fabric that is not comfortable to sleep with. If you keep the basics in mind, your quilt back will turn out to be just as good as the quilt top.

Binding the Quilt

The last step in your endeavor to create the quilt is binding. The thickness of the binding is around 0.5 inch and forms one of the most noticeable and dominant fabrics in your piece. You must choose the color of the binding rather carefully to ensure your quilt has a balanced look. For instance, if you have a yellow border and green blocks on your quilt, you can go for a green binding to put the quilt together.

It is not mandatory for you to use the same fabric for binding as the quilt fabric. You may use a different fabric and color for the purpose. However, the use of a plain-colored fabric is recommended. If the color of your quilt is bright, then you may use a black-colored binding. On the other hand, if the quilt is light-colored, white is the color to go for.

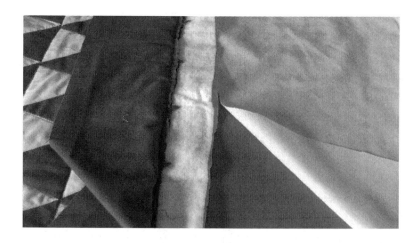

Chapter 6: Putting the Quilt Together

As you look to put the quilt together, you must look for a place where there is lots of space to work around. A kitchen slab or a large table in the living room is a great place to start. However, before you start, be sure to put a rug on the surface underneath the table so that anything you use like needles and threads do not fall on the floor.

If you are unable to find such a table, you can put a rug on the floor and start there and then. However, this can have a toll on your back. So, plan and work accordingly. If you plan to take this option, clear the floor and put a board or rug on the floor to keep your materials safe and intact.

Assembling the Quilt

Once you are ready, the first thing you need to do is to get the three layers of your quilt assembly in order. Therefore, place the backing, followed by the batting and finished on top by the quilt top. Be extremely careful while putting the assembly together. All the three layers need to be aligned perfectly.

The order of sizes should increase from backing to the quilt top. Therefore, your quilt top should be bigger than the batting, which in turn should be bigger than the backing. It is always good to have help from someone else in making this assembly and getting it right.

Pinning the Quilt

The next thing is to pin the sandwich together. Hold the three layers of the quilt and pin it up from the center of the quilt. Be careful not to disturb the alignment of the assembly in the process. Now, work along the lines of the squares and sashing and put a pin at every 6 inches. Smooth the fabric and batting as you move from the innermost area to the outermost area.

Tacking the Quilt

Once you have pinned your quilt together, you may either keep the pins as a base and work with the quilt or use tacking to get rid of the quilt. If you are using strong pins and plan to hand-stitch the quilt, you may choose to leave it as it is. However, with tacking, you will no longer have to worry about the displacement of the pins and the quilt falling apart.

Tacking is a process that requires you to place big running stitches from the middle to the top of the quilt top in the same order as the pins. Ideally, you must put one-inch stitches separated by a distance of 0.5 inches. These stitches are just grid lines that you will have to remove after you have completed the quilting process. It is good to perform this process using a thread of noticeable color in view of the fact that it will be much easier to get hold of the thread for removal at the end.

Regardless of the approach and method you plan to use for the quilting process, tacking gives your quilt the strength that keeps the quilt together during the quilting process. Moreover, you no longer have to worry about the puckering of the backing or bubbling of the quilt interior as you work on the quilt.

Tying the Quilt

In order to hold the sandwich of your quilt together, you can adopt one of the three techniques explained in this section. The simplest technique used for this purpose is tying knots at regular intervals throughout the length and breadth of the quilt. This technique is generally adopted for quilts that are heavier in batting and are difficult to sew across the quilt.

Whether you put knots on the top or the reverse side of the quilt, it is a matter of choice. If you are planning to put the knots on the quilt top, you will have to finish the knot with a tassel or a button to give it a beautiful look. You may also embroider the extra thread on the top into a pattern that beautifies the quilt top.

An important thing to note and remember here is that the thread you use for the tying purpose is the most essential aspect of your process. If you use a weak thread prone to breaking, the whole purpose will be defeated. Also, ensure you use threads that are colorfast. Using threads that require excessive aftercare can be troublesome, to say the least.

Ideally, this method of tying is used for quilts that are unconventional. Another important thing to consider here is the placement of knots. If you wish to use this quilt for everyday purposes, then the knots must be evenly distributed and higher in number, across the dimensions of the quilt to keep the same from wear and tear.

How to decide the placement of knots is usually a dilemma that most quilters face during these last phases of quilting. As a rule, you must follow the pattern you have used to create the quilt. For instance, if you have shaped patches, placing knots at the corners of each of the patches can be a great way to begin. However, if your pattern is asymmetric, you may end up with many knots in one area and less knots in another area. There is nothing wrong with this arrangement at all.

You will be constantly faced with the debate of whether hand-made quilts are better than machine-made quilts. While hand-made quilts have an authenticity that machine-made quilts can never even come close to, machine-made quilts are more precisely created and simpler to make. Most people who use machine-made quilts may even argue that machine-made quilts look the same and cost much less in terms of time and convenience.

The choice of which one to use is entirely yours and is usually dependent on a few factors. If you have the time and experience to pull off a hand-made quilt, then a hand-made quilt is the best option for you. However, if you lack the skill and are short on time, you can go for the machine-made option right away.

To help you make a choice, let's discuss the two tying techniques in greater detail. If you wish to give hand-made quilting a try, you will need to have thread, needle and a quilting hoop to start with. Depending on your skill level, the time required to complete a design may vary. There are several techniques that are followed for hand quilting. The most common of these techniques is to fit the hoop in the middle of the quilt to start with.

However, if you are using applique, going across each of the shapes is a much better idea. You can vary the puffiness of each shape depending on your preference and liking. The art here is to put small stitches evenly distributed and uniformly created. You will not be able to achieve this if you rush things. In the case of a patchwork quilt, you must start with the middle and follow the lines of the quilt for sections.

You may trace shapes and make lines you can follow as you quilt your piece. You may also use a process called stippling to make things easy for you. However, this method is usually adopted for quilts that have a heavy batting. During the process, the quilter creates an intricate sewing pattern made out of curves on the quilt. You may leave this out as a beginner. But as you gain experience, this is certainly something you can think of exploring.

Machine quilting is a quicker and convenient alternative to the laborious hand quilting. You no longer have to go through the painstaking methods of pushing the needle and thread across the three layers of the quilt. There are a variety of stitches and patterns available for machine quilting. The precision that cannot be achieved with hand quilting are possible with machine quilting. All the patterns and shapes will be flawlessly equal.

The usage of machines for quilting varies depending on the type of quilt. For instance, if you are creating an applique quilt, you will have to stitch the applique shapes by hand and then cover them up with machine stitches to hold the quilt firmly. Techniques like cross hatching and stippling are much simpler to achieve with the machine. However, like with any skill, you will get better at it with experience. The fundamental difference between hand quilting and machine quilting is that hand quilting is more of an art than a skill. However, machine quilting explores the skill aspect of quilting a little more than the artistic grade.

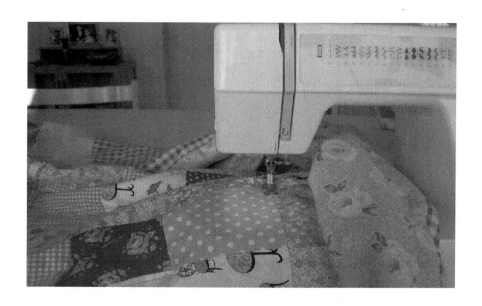

Binding a Quilt

Once you have reached the binding phase of quilt making, you can be assured your quilt is almost ready and all the hard work is about to pay off. However, hold your ground because it ain't over yet. This last step is one of the most crucial steps in the quilting process and can be performed in two different ways.

The first method used for binding the quilt is to pull the edges off the quilt top and backing and sewing them together. Although, this is a comparatively uncomplicated process and looks flawless, it is not as strong as the other process. Therefore, this is not a method you must adopt in case you are making the quilt for everyday use.

The second method of binding the quilt is to add another strip of fabric to the quilt called the binding. The fabric you use for this strip must be cut 0.5 inches wider than the length you need. Fold half of this strip material along the line of the backing and iron it. Next, place the quilt top over this folded binding and press again. Measuring the distance as 0.25 inches from the edge, sew on the quilt top and backing. Continue this process until all the edges are secured.

Once you have completed the process, your quilt is ready for use.

Conclusion

I hope the book was able to help you create a quilt of your own.

The next step is to use the information in this book.

Thank you and good luck!

57942451R00032

Made in the USA
Lexington, KY
29 November 2016